STORY BY DR HARMEET KAUR BHALLA

RANI LAXMIBAI OF JHANSI

BlueRose ONE.com
Stories Matter
NewDelhi • London

BLUEROSE PUBLISHERS
U.K.

BlueRose ONE.com
Stories Matter
NewDelhi • London

For permissions requests or inquiries regarding this publication, please contact:

BLUEROSE PUBLISHERS
www.BlueRoseONE.com
info@bluerosepublishers.com
+4407342408967

ISBN: 978-93-6783-993-5

Cover design: Daksh
Typesetting: Tanya Raj Upadhyay

First Edition: March 2025

RANI LAXMIBAI

Call her Manu or Manikarnika Tambe
The land of Benaras was hallowed
A fearless soul chuckled
In the lap of Bhagirathi

Chabili the frolicsome was raised
By Nana Sahib in Bithoor on the banks of Ganga
The petite girl flourished and was praised
Zealously riding, shooting and fencing

From Manu to Chabili to Laxmibai
She became an epitome of Goddess Saraswati
Raja Gangadhar became her groom
At thirteen she went into a swoon

She was born to fight
Strive for her rights
O! Women of Jhansi leave the cocoon
Save your country from the doom

A blossoming widow, an adopted child
The foe defamed her day and night
She shrieked to the English
"I will not give my Jhansi
I will not give my Jhansi"

In that gloomy fiery night
The dark clouds thundered
The fort was plundered
It was a devastating sight

Into the thin air she vanished
With her two soul companions
Anand Rao and Badal
She took her deadly stride

Her rivals followed her
She dared not to deter
But wounded she fell
For her dear ones her heart did swell

The city Jhansi and the country India she breathed for

She was born for Jhansi

She lived for Jhansi

She died for Jhansi.

From the book ‘Kohinoor’ written by Dr Harmeet Kaur Bhalla

RANI LAXMIBAI

Laxmibai was born on 19th November,1828 in Varanasi, a city in the state of Uttar Pradesh, India. She was born in a Marathi Karhade Brahmin family to parents Morapant Tambe and Bhagirathi Tambe. Her parents came from Tambe village of the Guhagar taluka located in the Ratnagiri district of the modern day Maharastra. Her father was a Commander during the war of Kalyanpranth.

She was initially named Manikarnika and affectionately Manu by her parents. Her, mother died when she was four years old while her father worked for Peshwa Baji Rao II of Bithoor District.

As a child her father noticed her over enthusiastic and playful behaviour. Her childhood was quite an uncommon one. She was more independent in her childhood than others of her age. During those days education was scarce with schools allowing only male participants so it became almost impossible for Manikarnika to gain education. Thus, she learned to read and write at home.

She was a relative of Nana Sahib the adopted son of the exiled Peshwa Baji Rao II. She was brought up in the Peshwa household which was quite an unusual upbringing for a Brahmin girl. She grew up with Nana Sahib and Tatya Tope at the Peshwas court. They noticed that she was different from other children. The, Peshwa named her 'Chhabili' as she was lively, jovial, and beautiful.

Since childhood she was very fond of elephants and horses.In one such incident Nana Sahib was riding on his elephant. When Manu saw him she made several requests as she too wanted to ride but to no avail. His refusal left a lasting impact on her. As a child she then declared that she would have ten elephants to every one elephant of Nana Sahib. She even once saved the life of Nana Sahib when his horse went out of control when she was seven years old.

She was trained with boys and became skilled in sword fighting and riding. She even learned archery, martial arts fencing and Malla Khamba. She practised all these with her childhood friends Tantya Tope and Nana Sahib. Since childhood her life had been full of ups and downs.

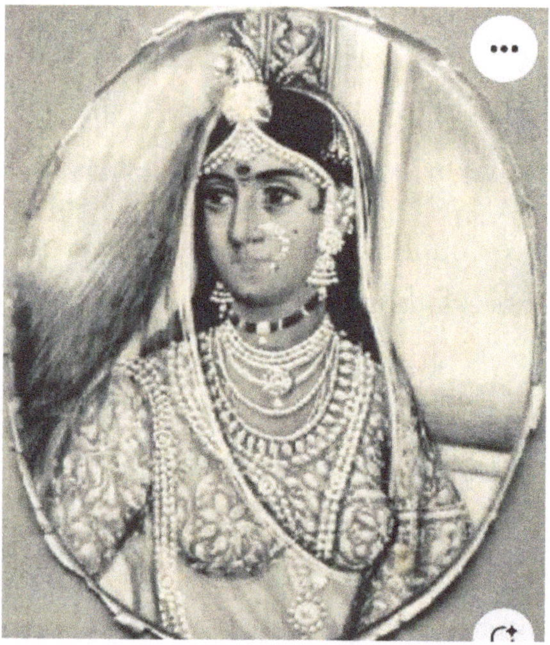

Rani Laxmibai

Gangadhar Rao Newalkar the fifth king of Jhansi was born in 1814.He was a Marathi Karhade Brahmin. He was the son of Shiv Rao Bhau and Padma Bai. The Britishers accepted him as the king in 1843.He was an able administrator and he improved the financial condition of Jhansi which had deteriorated during his predecessor's rule. He possessed considerable taste and some scholarship; he collected a fine library of Sanskrit manuscripts and enriched the architecture of the town of Jhansi. He was first married to Ramabai, who died soon after.

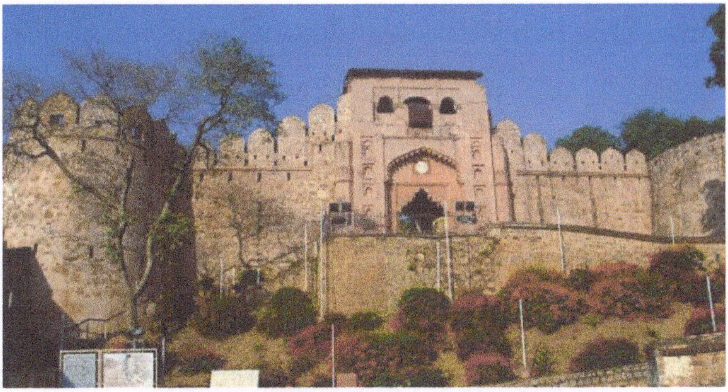

Jhansi fort

In May 1842 Manikarnika was married at the age of fourteen to Maharaja of Jhansi, Raja Gangadhar Rao Newalkar. Her marriage took place at the Shri Ganesh Temple in Jhansi which is located in the narrow by lanes of Jhansi's old city inside Ganesh Bazaar. The temple is ordinary yet unique in structure. It beholds the resplendent, marble idol of Lord Ganesh, his divine countenance radiates with grace and wisdom that transcends time itself.

It was here amidst the sacred rites and solemn rituals, that Manikarnika Tambe was anointed with the name 'Rani Lakshmibai,'a name that would echo through the annals of history as a beacon of courage and defiance against colonial oppression. She was named Laxmibai after marriage in honour of the Hindu goddess Devi Laxmi and according to the Maharashtrian tradition of women being given a new name after marriage. Rani Laxmibai became the queen of Jhansi after marriage.

She was welcomed warmly at the Jhansi Fort. It was a fortress situated on a large hilltop called Bangira. The fort has North Indian style of Fort construction. The granite walls of the fort were 16 to 20 feet thick and on the south side, the city walls met. The south face of the fort was almost perpendicular.

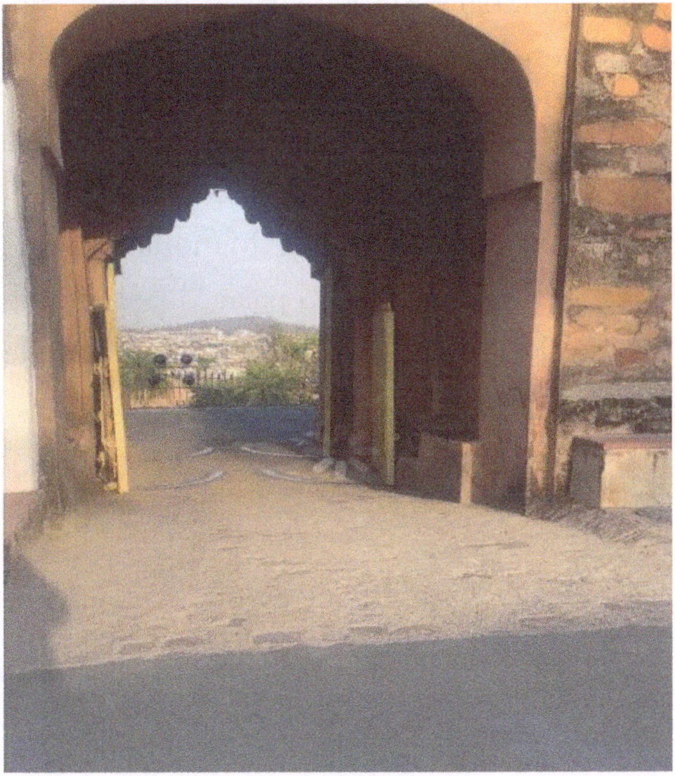

In the corner of the fort was the dark dingy Kal-Kothari where freedom fighters considered a threat were imprisoned. Adjacent to it was the Panch Mahal, the five-storey palace that looks immaculate, where the Rani resided with her husband Raja Gangadhar Rao. To the right end of the fort was a gate that went down towards Rani Lakshmibai's Amod Garden. Just opposite the Garden lies the Hanging Tower. Raja Gangadhar Rao used it to hang the criminals.

Rani Laxmibai's mother-in-law Sakku Bai took her to visit the Murli Manohar temple often. The temple is a grand palace like building where Lord Krishna is worshipped. The temple was the main centre of faith of the royal family.

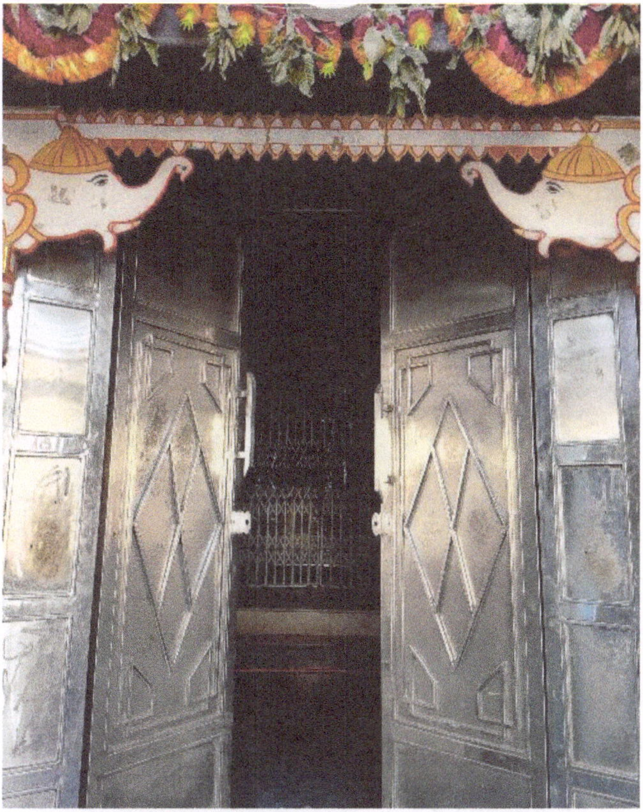

Murli Manohar

There were ten gates that gave access to the fort. These were Khanderao Gate, Datia Gate, Bhanderi Gate, Unnao Gate, Badagaon Gate, Laxmi Gate, Sagar Gate, Orchha Gate, Saiyar Gate and Chand Gate. Inside the fort was the Shiva temple constructed during the reign of Naroshankar(1742-1757)

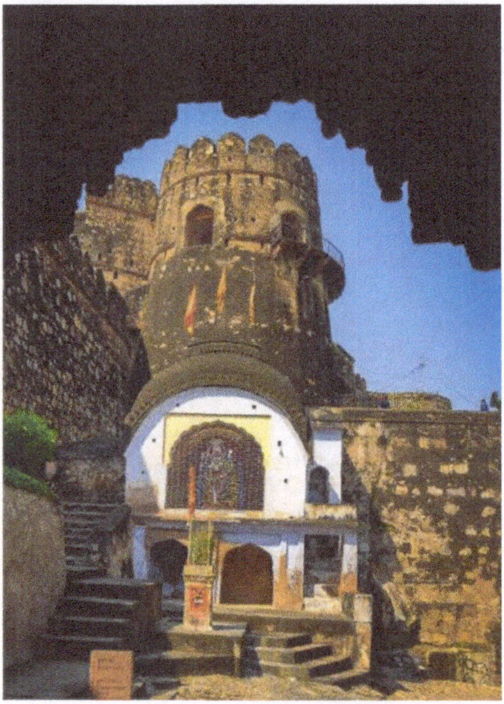

There is a Ganesha temple at the entrance where Rani did her daily prayers.

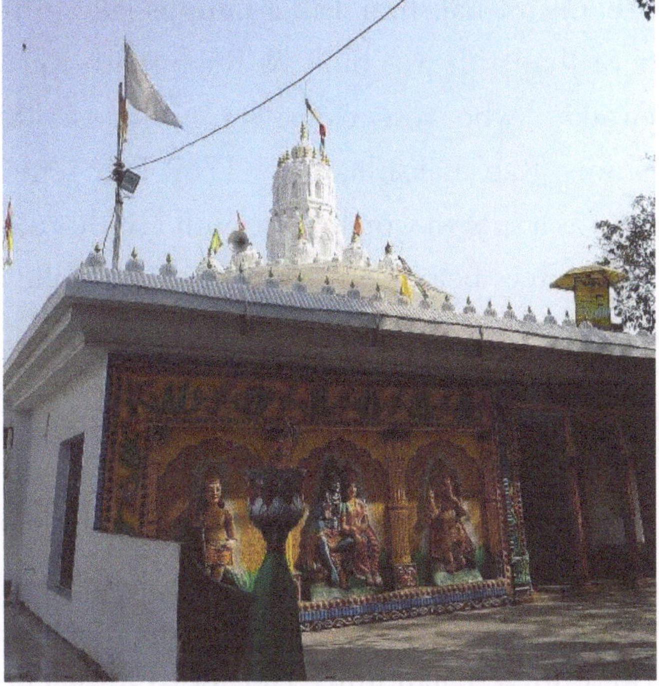

Mahalaxmi temple

The Baradari, a pavilion in the Jhansi fort was built by Maharaja Gangadhar Rao for his brother Raghunath Rao, who loved art and architecture. The Jharokas in the Baradari are similar to Hawa Mahal in Jaipur as they provide relief from summer heat. Rani Laxmi Bai visited the Mahalakshmi Temple daily. It is situated on the banks of Lakshmi Tal, a famous lake in the city of Jhansi. It was built by Raghunath Rao II Newalkar, who rose to power in Jhansi after Vishwas Rao Lakshman in 1769.The temple served as a spot of worship for both Hindu rulers and devotees belonging to the general public. It stands in honour of Goddess Lakshmi, the goddess of good fortune, wealth and prosperity according to the Hindu religion.

Rani Laxmibai was accustomed to riding on horseback accompanied by escorts between the palace and the temple. At times she was also carried in a palanquin. Her horses included Sarangi, Pavan, and Badal. She would exercise at weightlifting, wrestling, and steeplechasing before breakfast.

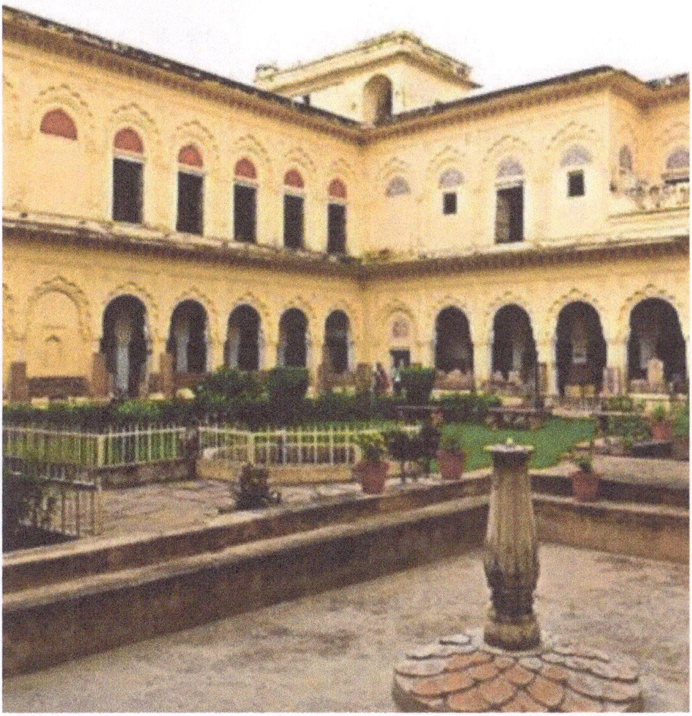

Rani Mahal

In September 1851 she gave birth to a baby boy who was named Damodar Rao. It was very tragic as her son died due to chronic illness when he was just four months old. Raja Gangadhar continued to be sick after his son's death.

Her husband Gangadhar Rao too died in 1853.Just a day before he died, he along with Rani Laxmibai adopted his cousin's Vasudev Newalkar of Parola's son Anand Rao, in presence of a British official. He wanted him to serve as his successor thus he was renamed Damodar Rao. The officer was given a letter stating that Jhansi's government was to be entrusted to his widow and his son should be given equal respect.

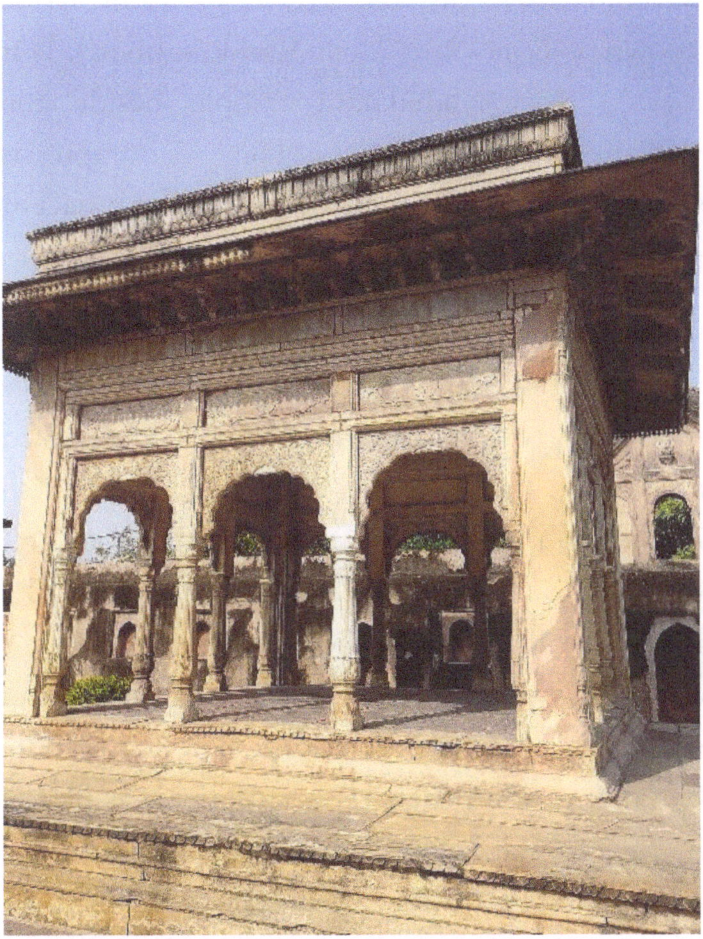

Samadhi of Maharaj

The Cenotaph of Raja Gangadhar Rao, The Raja of Jhansi, was built after his death by his queen Rani Laxmi Bai in 1853.It came to be known as Raja Gangadhar Rao ki Chhatri. It is located near Mahalaxmi temple beside the Laxmi lake in Jhansi. The Cenotaph is surrounded by a lush green garden, an adjacent pond and rich architectural designs.

After the death of her husband, Laxmibai went into a state of shock. Lord Dalhousie implemented the Doctrine of Lapse and staked a claim on the territories of Jhansi. The British refused to recognize her adopted son as an heir to the throne citing the Doctrine of Lapse. The British unfortunately did not recognise their child as a valid heir, thus the tenancy of the land was reverted to the overlord, The East India Company. Soon their representative was placed in the small kingdom to take care of administrative duties. When she was informed of this Rani Laxmibai cried out, "I shall not surrender my Jhansi,"(main apni Jhansi nahi doongi).

The British ruled Jhansi after the death of her husband. In 1854, the Rani was presented with a yearly pension of Rs 60,000 and told to vacate the place and fort. Rani Laxmibai the widow of the king petitioned the Governor General and the British Government that Damodar Rao's claim to the throne should be recognized, however, this petition was rejected. She moved into a place called Rani Mahal which is now a museum.

After being expelled from her palace, Laxmibai continued to live in Rani Mahal. The Rani Mahal or the Queen's Palace was built by Raghu Nath -II of the Newalkar family (1769-96) subedar of Jhansi. Regarding its architecture, it is a flat-roofed, two-storeyed building having a quadrangular courtyard with a small well and one fountain on opposite sides. The palace has six halls and parallel corridors with multi-foiled arches and a number of small rooms. The Darbar Hall, approached by a flight of steps, is beautifully decorated with paintings in bright colours exhibiting various flowers, animals and geometrical motifs. The arches are embellished with peacock and rosette patterns. The ground floor of the palace houses sculptures collected from Madanpur, Barua Sagar, Dudhai and Chandpur dating from the Gupta to Medieval periods.

She was firm about protecting Jhansi from British annexation. Laxmibai began securing her position and formed an army of both men and women who were given military training in fighting a battle. Several women joined her army. Women of her army were taught military tactics, physical fitness and marksmanship.

Jhalkaribai was a close confidante who rose through the ranks in Rani's army and commanded her own troops. She was the commander of the Durga Dal, or women's brigade, in Rani Laxmibai's army. She was a prominent advisor to the Rani and was known for disguising herself as the queen to fool the British. The other women warriors who accompanied were Moti Bai, and Kashi Bai. Her women were given the training to carry ammunition and supply food to the soldiers.

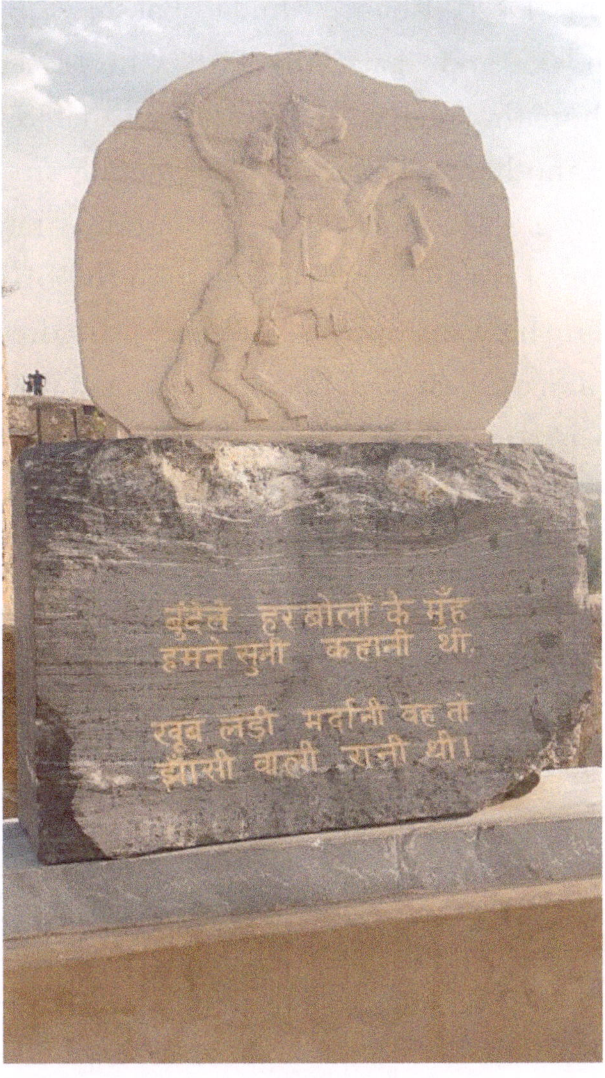

Inside Jhansi fort

The other warriors included Gulam Gaus Khan, Dost Khan, Khuda Baksh, Sundar Mundar, and Lala Bhau Bakshi. Deewan Raghunath Singh and Deewan Jawahar Singh were another great warrior. She carefully studied the geography of her kingdom, and the strategic points of the Sikh army's fight with the British. When she went out on horseback, she dressed like a man, wearing a metallic helmet, a flowing turban, a metallic plate, pajamas, and a sash. On both sides she carried pistols, and daggers. In addition, she carried a sabre. Along with these warriors the local population too joined Rani Laxmibai irrespective of their religion or caste whenever the need arose. They were ready to sacrifice their lives for independent India and Rani.

After the revolt of 1857 Laxmibai was declared ruler of Jhansi and she became Rani Laxmibai. She ruled on behalf of her minor heir.

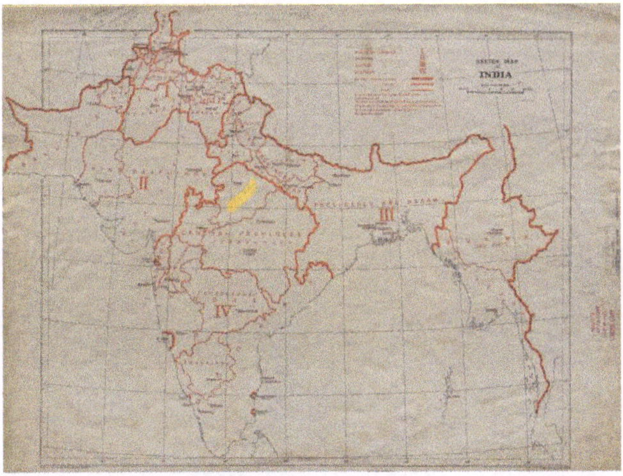

On May 10th,1857 the Indian rebellion started in Meerut. When the news reached Jhansi, Lakshmi Bai increased her protection and conducted a Haldi Kumkum ceremony to convince the people that the British were cowards and there's no need to fear them.

In June 1857, the Rani took over the administration of Jhansi after the British were killed by Indian troops. In August 1857 allies of the British attacked Jhansi. Lakshmibai set up a foundry to cast cannons within the premises of the Jhansi fort. Fire from the cannons were directed at the enemy forces from the walls of the fort.

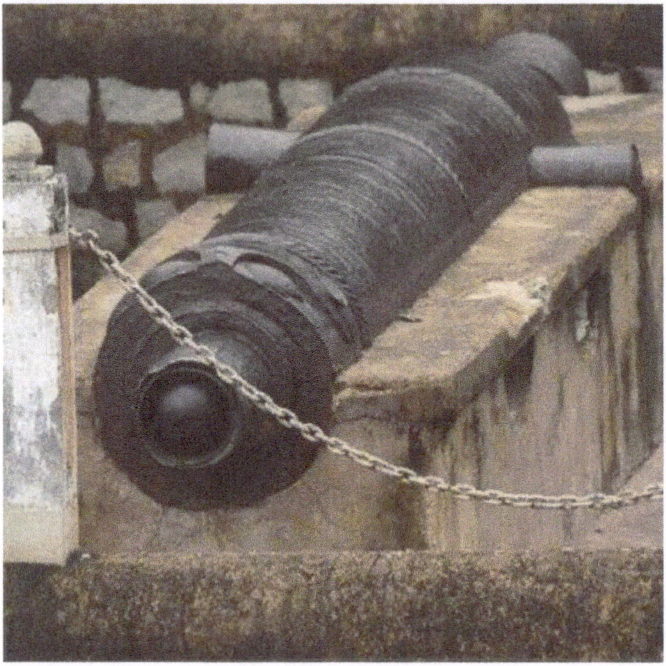

Kadak Bijli Canon

The 'Kadak Bijli' Cannon that evidently thundered on firing was placed at the entrance. It was operated by Gulam Gaus Khan. The 'Bhawani Shankar' Cannon was handled by Moti Bai the woman gunner. The front portion of the canon has the shape of a crocodile and the back portion has elephant inscribed on it. It was believed to be blessed by Goddess Bhawani.

From August 1857 to January 1858 Jhansi under Rani Laxmibai's rule was at peace. The British had announced that troops would be sent to maintain control but none of them arrived. This strengthened the position of Rani Laxmibai's party as they wanted to flee the British. When the British forces finally arrived in March they found it well defended and the fort had heavy guns which could fire over the town and nearby countryside.

On March 23rd 1858, Sir Hugh Rose, the commanding officer of the British demanded Rani to surrender the city and warned that if she refused the city will be destroyed. Laxmibai refused and proclaimed "We fight for independence. Lord Krishna said that if we are victorious, we will enjoy the fruits of victory. If defeated and killed on the battlefield, we shall gain eternal glory and salvation."

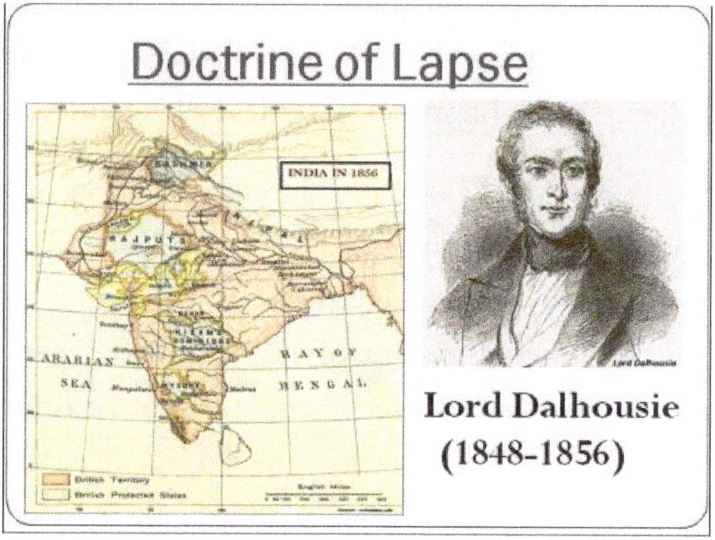

On March 24,1858, the British forces bombarded Jhansi. The defenders of Jhansi sent an appeal to Laxmibai's childhood friend Tatya Tope. He responded to this request and sent more than 20,000 soldiers to fight against the British army. During the battle with Tatya Tope's forces, part of the British forces continued the siege and by 2nd April it was decided to assault by a breach in the walls. Four columns assaulted the defences at different points and those attempting to scale the walls came under heavy fire. Two other columns entered the city and palace together. The soldiers failed to relieve Jhansi. Finally in March 1858, the British re captured Jhansi after a strong resistance.

Her fort was captured from all four sides but Rani fled with her horse Badal and her son Damodar Rao tied on the back. She escaped the British forces as she jumped off the fort's wall on a horseback. The drop was 20 feet and the landing a steep downward incline. They survived but the horse died. The Rani escaped in the night with her son, surrounded by guards. The escort included the warriors Khuda Baksh Basharat Ali(commandant), Ghulam Gaus Khan, Dost Khan, Lala Bhau Bakshi, Moti Bai, Sunder-Munder, Kashi Bai, Deewan Raghunath Singh and Deewan Jawahar Singh.

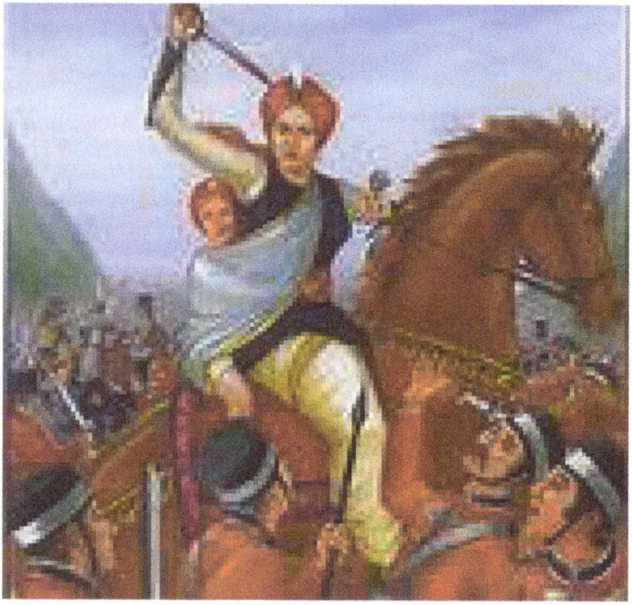

Along with young Damodar Rao, the Rani decamped to Kalpi along with her forces where she joined other rebel forces including those of Tantya Tope. On May 22nd,1858, British forces attacked Kalpi and Lakshmi Bai was defeated. Then Rani Lakshmi Bai, Rao Sahib, and Tantya Tope fled to Gwalior.

On 17th June in Kotah-ki- Serai near Phool Bagh in Gwalior the British under Captain Heneage fought the large Indian force commanded by Rani Laxmibai who was trying to leave the area. The three of them wanted to occupy the Gwalior fort due to its strategic importance. The British slaughtered 5000 Indian soldiers and any Indian above the age of sixteen. The rebel forces occupied the city without facing any opposition and proclaimed Nana Saheb as Peshwa of Maratha dominion and Rao Sahib as his governor. On June 16th Rani Laxmibai fought bravely but she was attacked by one of the hussars; she was unhorsed and wounded in the battle probably by his sabre. Shortly afterwards as she sat bleeding by the roadside, she recognized the soldier and fired him with a pistol, whereupon he "dispatched the young lady with his carbine".

She died on 18th June,1858 while fighting against the British at Gwalior. She was dressed as a soldier when she died. She was cremated as per her wishes, near the local people. She had said that the British should never touch her body thus one of her maids helped in organising a fast funeral. It is assumed her funeral was held on the same day. Her tomb is located in the Phool Bagh area of Gwalior.

The British captured the city of Gwalior after three days. In the British report of the battle Hugh Rose commented that Rani Laxmibai is "personable, clever and beautiful," and she is the most dangerous of all Indian leaders. He even noted, "Here lay the woman who was the only man among the rebels."

Her father Moropant Tambe was hanged a few days after Jhansi's fall. Her adopted son Damodar Rao lived in a pitiful state although he received a grant from the British Raj.

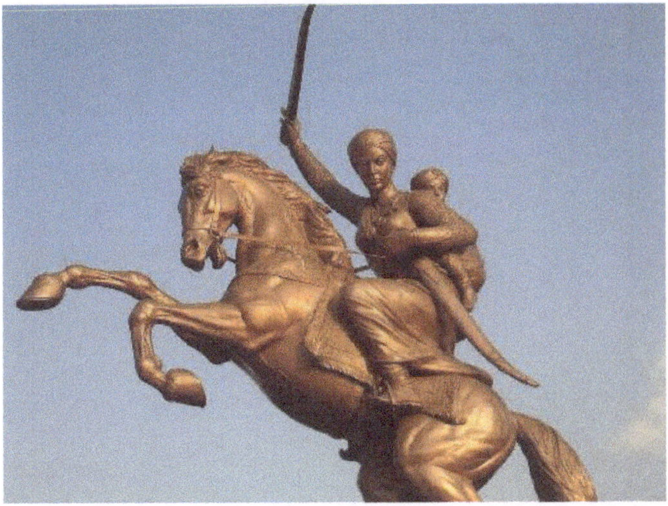

She is called The Joan of Arc of India. There have been very few women in the history of India who sacrificed their lives for the sake of their country and Rani Laxmibai was one of them. She instilled the feelings of patriotism in the hearts of her fellow men and women. She is always remembered for laying the foundation stone of women empowerment in India. Her story of bravery, and unwavering dedication to justice shall be remembered for the years to come.